The Brown Brothers of Milawa Wine and Food Book

This book is dedicated to the memory
of our dear friend and colleague Tom Seabrook,
a man whose gentle erudition and boundless enthusiasm
for wine and food we all miss greatly.

The Brown Brothers of Milawa Wine and Food Book.

The Brown Brothers wish to thank
these special friends for the production of this book.
Tom Seabrook, John Newton, Peter Longhurst, James Bell,
Tandy Rowley, Kate Frost, Jean Frost, David Frost.

First published in Australia by The Brown Brothers
Milawa Vineyard Pty Ltd, Milawa VIC, 3678, Australia.

First edition July 1986 reprinted March 1988

ISBN 1 86252 302 9

Printed and bound in Australia by
The Pot Still Press, 41-43 Dickson Avenue, Artarmon, Sydney, 2064.

Rhine Riesling

Contents.

Introduction.

This book is a guide to the very real pleasures to be derived from matching good wine with good food.

It is not a rule book. There are no hard and fast rules for matching food and wine. Merely guidelines, most of them based on commonsense, with sound gastronomic and aesthetic reasons behind them. To break them, it helps to know them.

And, of course, breaking old rules and making new ones is what we must do constantly. Nothing has changed more in the last twenty years than the way we Australians eat and drink.

Apart from anything else, we probably choose from a greater diversity of national cuisines than any other people on earth, with the possible exception of New Yorkers.

Alongside the ever-present Chinese, you are just as likely to find French, Italian, Greek, Spanish, Lebanese, Japanese, Vietnamese and Indian restaurants. In Sydney, there is even an establishment offering a mixture of African and Sri Lankan food.

What appears to be emerging from this mixing pot is a national cuisine as delightfully varied as our origins; a style of cooking dubbed by one of its most famous exponents, Gay Bilson, 'upstart cuisine'.

From the quiet seclusion of our vineyards and winery at Milawa, we have been noting and absorbing these changes since 1889. The last twenty years, however, have seen an acceleration of the pace that has left us, at times, breathless.

As if to match this diversity of food choices, our winemakers produce a greater variety of wine flavours and types than perhaps any other winemaking nation. The reasons for this are worth examining briefly.

Firstly, as a relatively late starter in winemaking, Australia is not bound by ancient tradition and proscription.

The French system of appellation control, while admirably protecting quality and type, is restrictive to the innovative winemaker. A wine for a certain district, to achieve the 'Apellation Contrôlée' status, must obey rules concerning permitted grape varieties, quantities of varieties in blends, alcohol level, and the viticultural and vinicultural process.

Australia, presenting totally different climatic conditions and problems, could not be expected to produce wines in exactly the way they are made in Europe.

Free from bureaucratic restrictions, encouraged by new technology, our winemakers can experiment with totally new winemaking ideas.

We only need to cast our eyes across the shelves of a large wine merchant to see the results of this period of bold innovation and experimentation.

It is important to note, then, even in the midst of such culinary and oenological upheavals, much does not change. The advice of the Roman farmer/poet Virgil to the winegrower that 'vines love an open hill' is as true today as it was 2000 years ago; as is the assertion of the Australian farmer/poet Eric Rolls that 'the final flavour of wine should always be fruit'.

And, stripped of malarkey and mystique, that is exactly what wine is. The fermented juice of the fruit from any one of the hundreds of varieties grapevines grown.

This fermented juice is prepared by a winemaker – part scientist, part artist, part farmer, part alchemist – to bring out its flavour, and then often left in bottles or barrels in a cool dark place for Time (another alchemist) to work mysterious changes to that flavour.

The resultant liquid, from pale straw to deep purple in colour, is called wine. And it has the ability to loosen tongues, gladden hearts, make ordinary food taste wonderful, and wonderful food, sublime.

Mondeuse

Introducing The Brown Family

Standing from left to right, Ross, Peter, Jan, John Snr, June, Roger.
Seated, Judy, John Snr, Pat, Elu.

The first member of the Brown family to plant grapes for winemaking at Milawa was John Francis Brown. He began his first planting in 1885. In 1889 he made the first vintage.

The original property is still in use, and the Canadian style barn built in 1860 and used as the first winery, is today used to age fortified wines in wood.

The enterprise flourished. By 1900, a larger winery was needed to accommodate the increase in production. And then, in 1915, disaster struck. The phylloxera infection that swept through the district all but wiped out John Francis Brown. But he hung on, and replanted with phylloxera resistant Californian rootstock. By 1920, the vineyard was again flourishing.

In 1933, after leaving school, John Charles Brown joined his father. In 1984, John Brown Senior, as he is known today, celebrated his fiftieth vintage.

Then, as now, John Brown Senior loved the countryside of North East Victoria — flanked by the King and Ovens rivers and bounded by the Murray River to the North, the Victorian Alps to the South and East. But when he began to work with his father, he began to look at the countryside of his childhood in a new light.

The area had always been renowned for its fortified wines. Gradually, John Brown Senior began to realise it had the potential for much more.

He was one of the first winemakers in the area to recognise the potential of the area's quite remarkable climatic diversity for the cultivation of more varieties of grapes than had previously been thought possible.

He began to experiment. And, over the years, growing different varieties in various pockets of the countryside, discovered ideal combinations of grape and soil, climate and altitude.

Over the intervening fifty years, John Brown married, and he and his wife Pat raised four sons. They have all since joined the family enterprise. The eldest, John Graham Brown, is the winemaker. Peter Brown is the viticulturist, Ross is in charge of marketing and sales, and the youngest, Roger, propagation and the continuing science of developing new varieties.

The entire family lives in and around the beautiful countryside of North East Victoria. All have their roles to play in the growing of grapes, and the making and selling of wine.

No other winemaking family in Australia has contributed more to the development of varietal winemaking and grape growing techniques.

And, of course, like all families dedicated to wine, they share an abiding interest in the food that is to be eaten with that wine.

This book, then, is the distillation of almost one hundred years of one family's dedication to the art of winemaking, and the pleasures of the table.

Tasting Wine.

Of the considerable quantities of wine consumed, very little is actually tasted. Most goes into the mouth and down the throat before it's had time to release any flavour at all.

It's almost as if the fear of being thought a 'wine snob' deters many from taking the time and care to taste the wine they drink.

There is nothing mysterious about winetasting. No equipment needed other than a glass. And nothing special to do other than to pay attention to colour, aroma and taste, and then to remember what you like.

The most important organ of wine appreciation is the nose, followed by the brain. Most of what we taste, we taste through our sense of smell. The tongue perceives only whether a taste is sweet or sour, salty or bitter.

To reach the brain, where the more subtle tastes are registered and recognised, the vapours of wine need to be inhaled through the nose, or from behind the soft palate at the back of the mouth, where they are dissolved in moisture, and transported to the *olfactory bulb*.

This is the taste centre of the brain, situated just in front of the *temporal lobe*, which, among other functions, acts as the brain's 'memory bank'. It is here that the tastes are registered, and recalled.

When tasting a wine, the first impression of interest is the colour. A honey gold tinge to a Rhine Riesling, for example, indicates a wine with a little age on it

Now for a moment of real pleasure: the first inhalation of the bouquet and aroma of the wine. Taking care to concentrate, lift the glass to the nose and inhale deeply. A great deal of information is conveyed by this first deep whiff; the fruity aroma indicating the grape variety, a heady bouquet of age.

Now take a good mouthful. Encourage the wine to spill into every corner of the mouth, taking care to allow it to float to the back of the mouth, where it will reach the brain via the soft palate. Taking some air between the teeth, swill the wine and warm it in the mouth which will aid the release of its volatile esters. The full complement of sensations explode in the brain: richness, age, subtlety, varietal taste, undertones and overtones: in short, the quality of the wine.

At this point, having made a decision, the professional winetaster will spit the wine out. During the course of a tasting that might involve twenty wines, swallowing could prove disastrous. We lesser mortals are encouraged to do so.

Of course to treat every sip of wine to this process would be to bring conversation to a standstill. But once every component of a wine has been taken note of, each subsequent sip is far more enjoyable.

With practise, you will quite easily distinguish between the varietal flavours of the grapes; the peppery taste of Shiraz, the blackcurrant reminiscent of Cabernet Sauvignon, the luscious honeyed botrytis in a Noble Riesling.

Before closing this section, a short discussion of temperature. Nothing will ruin the taste of wine more than serving it too warm, or too cool.

The temperature for serving red wine is usually described as 'room'. This will mean one thing in Hobart, and quite another in Alice Springs. Served too cold, red wine will lose its flavour. Too warm, the alcohol begins to vaporise and the wine emits a heady smell that masks the flavour. 18°C (65°F) is usually taken as ideal, which, in our climate, may mean a short spell in the refrigerator before serving.

Likewise, a white wine served too cold will be 'unbalanced', the cold masking the flavour. Too warm, and the volatile flavour components will totally overwhelm the wine. A good midpoint is around 10°C (50°F).

Of course individual varieties within the red/white spectrum, as well as individual preferences, play a large part in deciding. Experimenting with your favourite wines is better than slavishly following formulae.

The French and the Spanish can teach us something about experimentation. The French propensity for chilling the light and more aromatic red wines for summer drinking, particularly those of the Beaujolais region, is only now being taken up with enthusiasm by Australian drinkers. For years, the Spanish have sipped their Sherries, particularly those from Manzanilla, chilled as an aperitif, often accompanied by olives stuffed with anchovies.

We will end this chapter with one rule that is absolutely unbreakable. The best wine is the one you enjoy drinking.

Merlot

Sauvignon Blanc

Serving

It was the French scientist Louis Pasteur who established the exact nature of the relationship between oxygen and wine.

The French wine merchants of the time had asked Napoleon III for help in discovering why so much of their product went bad before it reached the consumer. Napoleon passed the request on to Pasteur.

After conducting a series of experiments, he determined that while too much contact with oxygen was detrimental in that it encouraged the production of vinegar bacteria, a little oxygen was not only beneficial but necessary to wine production.

The action of oxygen on wine is gradual. And, in small quantities, it reacts with the esters, pigments and alcohol to create the complex flavours and bouquets of a great wine.

Which, of course, makes the simple act of pulling a cork on a bottle of wine one fraught with possibilities and dangers. Nevertheless we shall throw caution to the winds, and push ahead with the mechanics.

Firstly, the lead capsule covering the wine needs to be cut away from the lip so as not to come into contact with pouring wine. Use a knife or the blade on the corkscrew known as 'the waiter's friend'. Wipe any mould or dirt off the lip of the bottle and the top of the cork.

Using a good corkscrew, the simpler the better, remove the cork firmly and carefully.

In a restaurant you may be presented with the cork. If so, inspect the moist end, sniff it. It should smell sweetly of wine if the bottle has been stored correctly, laid on its side.

At home, merely check the cork for faults. If an old red has been opened, the cork should be hard and dark unless the bottle has been recently re-corked. If wine is oozing through the cork, check the wine in the bottle for signs of oxidation. If pieces of cork fall into the bottle, you'll be spared the decision to decant or not; you must decant to strain off the cork. Likewise if the cork crumbles, you should strain to get rid of the powdery cork. Use a silver strainer in preference, or a clean coffee filter paper.

If the wine has oozed, or the cork crumbled, first sniff the wine, then taste it. If it is 'off', it will taste or smell more like vinegar than wine. An 'off' wine is very rare these days, but not unheard of. Good restaurants or wine merchants will be only too happy to exchange your bottle.

Shiraz

If the cork is fine, and the bottle is open the decision is now whether or not to decant. That is, whether you believe the wine needs to breathe a little oxygen before it is drunk. Here, we are talking mainly about old red wines, although old whites may also need decanting.

Of course if you are organising the wine for a dinner, and you have decided to decant, you will have opened it anything from one to six hours ahead of time.

There are two main schools of thought about decanting. The first says, decant everything. The theory goes that contact with the air will work rapidly and effectively to bring any wine to its peak. The question is, how long should it be left before drinking? A good rule of thumb is the more full bodied the wine, the longer it needs.

The other point of view holds that only some wines and those which have spent a long time in the bottle especially, need to be opened out in a decanter.

Your taste must be the final judge. Experiment with some of your favourite wines. You may find that they improve noticeably after a couple of hours in a decanter.

A further reason to decant, besides the cork problem, is to remove sediment. In itself, sediment is no bad thing, merely evidence of bottle ageing.

If you do decide to decant, do so into a wide mouthed glass or crystal decanter. If in doubt, decant late. A good wine could 'flatten out' if left too long in the decanter. On the other hand, it can always be encouraged to open up by being swirled in the glass.

Decanting can, of course, be a ritual and some of us enjoy rituals. You may like to go all the way and arm yourself with a selection of decanters, a silver pouring funnel, and a decanting candelabrum (to illuminate sediment). If, on the other hand, you enjoy drinking more than ritual, just open the wine an hour or so before drinking.

Sylvaner

Wine and Food.

And now to the heart of the matter. The union of wine and food. We began this book by suggesting that, while most rules are made to be broken, there are some with sound chemical reasons for being. A case in point is that of red wine and fish.

All foods and all wines have a predominant sensuous characteristic. The refreshing and appetising characteristic of white wine is acid. The flavour of fish is predominantly salty. The acids in white wine enhance the flavour of fish, while the saltiness of fish emphasises the fruity grape flavours of white wine.

Conversely, the 'edge' of a good red wine is tannin, an astringent vegetable compound that reacts to the salt in the fish by leaving a bitter and metallic taste in the mouth.

That said, there are instances where this rule may be flouted. Tarrango, a light red wine made from a grape developed in Australia, of exceptional fruitiness, and best drunk fresh and chilled, teams admirably with such seafood as smoked salmon, smoked trout and mussels. These are the exceptions that prove the rule.

More often than not it makes more sense, both aesthetically and gustatorily, to drink a hearty red wine with a hearty red meat dish, and a cool white or golden wine with seafood. The flavours and the colours are complementary.

There are other rules, with similar grounding in flavour compatibility. Red wine does not really go with chocolate, nor, for some arcane reason, with artichokes. Vinegar in a salad dressing can play havoc with the taste of any wine, so take care.

The more we drink wine with various foods, the more we learn for ourselves which foods and wines are made for each other and which 'kill' each other. It is merely a question of paying attention to taste, flavour, aroma, to the more delightful combinations we discover, and remembering to consign to the scrap heap the more disastrous mistakes.

An elegant Shiraz that combines particularly well with rich game, duck, pheasant or squab may be too elegant for a hearty beef wellington.

The robustness of a Cabernet Sauvignon may stand up well to a strongly flavoured Greek stifato, but be totally swamped by a hot Madras curry.

The spice in Gewürztraminer works very well with most chinese food (excepting the fiery dishes of Szechuan) but could prove too complex for a delicately herbed roast chicken.

These are not rules, but principles, the results of experiments, your reactions to your experience. As anyone, having invited a disparate group to dinner and watched the most unlikely friendships blossom will confirm, you just never can tell.

Good wines before great, white before red, light before full bodied, dry before sweet and young before old are the basic rules for the order of wine through a dinner; although you will break them with great pleasure by serving a glass of honey sweet Noble Riesling with dessert, or a cleansing glass of champagne at the conclusion of a great meal.

This is a delicate subject to bring up, but it is a good idea, before opening a precious bottle of wine you've been saving for the occasion, consider the guest list. Nothing is more disconcerting than to see your treasure being guzzled like beer at the football.

Follow your nose, match flavours and pay attention to preferences, and you really can't go wrong. After all, we make wine to be tasted and enjoyed, not discussed and criticised.

Pinot Noir

Crouchen

Cooking with Wine.

Wine is used in cooking to add richness, flavour and succulence. Rarely should it be used to add the flavour of the wine itself, but rather to enhance the natural flavours of the food with which it is cooked.

The right variety of wine to drink with a dish is usually the wine to use in its cooking; although if you plan to serve a rare old wine with the meal, a more recent and inexpensive example will suffice for cooking. On the whole, however, cooking wine should be drinkable. If the dish is to be good enough to eat, the wine should be good enough to drink.

In cooking with wine, it is the flavour and not the alcohol that is being added. To achieve this, reduce the amount of wine by half by boiling, or simmer the dish in an open vessel.

Reduced wine may be kept in sealed bottles in the refrigerator for future use, as may any leftover wines. Reseal and if possible decant into smaller bottles to reduce surface contact with the air. Before using a leftover wine for cooking, taste it to ensure it hasn't gone off.

Various dregs of leftover red wine can be collected and bottled together for use as a marinade. Never underestimate the tenderising effect on meat of a couple of hours marinating in wine.

Oil, herbs and spices can be added to the marinade to enhance flavour. A leg of mutton marinated for a couple of days in red wine then baked with rosemary and garlic is magnificent and known in many countries as 'mock venison'.

A left over (but not off) white wine may be used to replace vinegar in salad dressing.

To make a delicious wine sauce for roast or fried meat, deglaze the pan juices with a little brandy, then douse with leftover red wine and reduce. If the sauce is a little grey, add a dash of tomato puree.

A beautiful garnish for grilled chops or pan fried calf's liver, wine merchant's butter, is made by reducing a little leftover red wine by half in a pan with chopped onion, fresh or dried thyme and a scrap of bayleaf. Strain and press, then blend with butter, parsley and chopped garlic. This can be frozen and used when needed.

Fish and shellfish can be poached in a court bouillon made by barely covering the fish with water, adding a quarter as much again white wine, diced carrot and finely chopped onion, or celery and leek with a bouquet garni and simmered for 30 minutes.

Mussels can be boiled in bulk or left over white wine instead of water, with a little finely chopped onion.

Try adding Port or Madeira to robust soups just before serving.

Or whipping Tokay, Muscat or Madeira through cream over fruit for dessert. Or poaching pears in red wine, or peaches in white wine.

Once you begin to use wine in your cooking, you will discover your own tricks, and formulate your own rules. We would like to leave this section with a suggestion for those of you with gardens who grow your own melons.

When picking the melon, leave a good 30 centimetres (about one foot) of stalk. Insert this into a bottle of port. Leave the melon to sip on the Port for a day or two. Chill and eat. A dessert fit for an Emperor.

Chardonnay

Entrées and Hors-d'oeuvres.

Here we begin to note some of those changes we mentioned earlier. It was not that long ago (perhaps fifteen vintages past) that the structure of a meal was carved in stone.

After an aperitif (in Anglo Saxon households usually a Sherry) came the soup (Brown Windsor) the entrée (fish) the main course (joint and two veg) and pudding (roly poly, spotted dick or stewed fruit and ice cream) followed by coffee and cheese.

With the entrée a white wine of indeterminate parentage and origin usually called 'hock' with the main course a similarly anonymous red wine, a 'claret' or a 'burgundy', and with the cheese, port: for the gentleman only, of course.

While this unvarying ritual did make the business of entertaining relatively easy for the host and hostess, its unvarying monotony did not give much to look forward to with surprise or delight.

The names at the top of this page, inherited as are many of our ancient gastronomic customs from the French, imply a similar rigid structure. Fortunately, this is not the case today. A meal may consist of two or more entrées. Hors-d'oeuvres may replace the entrée entirely, or, if the entertainment is a night long party, they may replace the meal altogether.

What these names do imply is the prelude to a meal. And whether your prelude is taken casually in the living room (hors-d'oeuvres) or formally at the dining table (entrée) the meal should have a beginning, a middle and an end. How you plan these three components is, of course, left entirely up to you.

You may still like to serve Sherry with hors-d'oeuvres, however you may like to serve it in the Spanish manner, lightly chilled; far more sensible in summer. Wine as an aperitif is becoming more popular; try one of the more aromatic whites, a Dry White Frontignac perhaps, or a Gewürztraminer with a handful of nuts and olives, or a platter of raw vegetables accompanied by a fresh mayonnaise or aioli.

The French are in the habit of serving a 'dessert wine' with paté or terrine as an entrée; try a Noble Riesling or a late harvest Orange Muscat & Flora with a bowl of chicken pâté.

Any of the crisp finishing whites will freshen and stimulate the palate; Rhine Riesling, Sauvignon Blanc or Chenin Blanc.

The idea behind the opening to the meal is that it should tantalise rather than satiate, and, like a good entertainer, leave you wanting more.

Seafood.

Basically, any good young dry white wine combines well with seafood. On closer examination, however, there is a wide variety of flavours to match within this general category.

The seatangy simplicity of natural oysters demands the crisp acidity of a Colombard, or the complexity of a Semillon, whose fruit character will be enhanced by the saltiness of the oysters.

The sweetness of lobster or crab can be complemented by a fruity wine, a Rhine Riesling, or perhaps even a Chenin Blanc, or contrasted with the flintiness of a wood aged Colombard or Chardonnay.

These two varietals will also team well with smoked fish; trout, mackerel, salmon or eel.

When cooking fish with a sauce, or in a hearty bouillabaisse type stew, the character of the sauce or the predominant flavour will determine the wine to accompany it. The spice of a Gewürztraminer with a fish stew, for example, or the full flavour and acidity of Sylvaner with fish mornay.

With a simple grilled Schnapper or Jewfish, nothing could be more compatible than a fresh young Rhine Riesling. Colombard teams well with mussels, and Sauvignon Blanc with Barramundi or John Dory.

If you're in the habit of squeezing lemon juice on fish or seafood, a more acid wine will make a better accompaniment: A Colombard or a Rhine Riesling for example.

Finally, should you enjoy drinking sweet wine with seafood, that then is the right wine for you.

There is such a rich variety of seafoods and white wines in Australia, that the possibilities for point and counterpoint, complement and contrast are as seemingly endless and varied as the coastline itself.

Chenin Blanc

Colombard

Meat.

Cabernet
Sauvignon

Now we come to discuss those wines that are, to many winelovers, the most satisfying. The great red wines of Australia. From the full bodied and flavoursome to the light and elegant, the best of them have proved themselves in competition and in the hearts and mouths of winedrinkers everywhere amongst the world's finest.

Let it be said at the outset, however, if you just plainly don't like red wine, a wood aged Chardonnay or Semillon provides an excellent accompaniment to roast beef or grilled steak. Drink and eat what you like. But every now and then, do try to cultivate a taste for red wine. You don't know what you're missing.

There are really only two guidelines to be acknowledged when matching red wine with meat. Firstly, the more intense the flavour, the more full bodied the wine; and secondly, save the finest for the plainest.

If you have a venerable old Cabernet Sauvignon or Shiraz slumbering in your cellar, the time to uncork/decant it is with a perfectly pinked eye fillet adorned by nothing more than a dob of English mustard.

At a barbecue, enjoy your grilled beef and bangers with mouthfulls of robust young Cabernet Sauvignon or Shiraz.

Perhaps the most versatile of the red wine grapes is the remarkable Pinot Noir. Lightly chilled, Pinot Noir is fruity enough to accompany spicy sausages; at room temperture, it's smooth and elegant enough to be drunk with your finest roasted leg of lamb or game dish.

Pork, depending upon how it is cooked, can be eaten with either red or white wine. A rich roast leg of pork with apple sauce will work equally well with Merlot or a Chardonnay.

With your favourite stews or meat recipes, experiment with the various red blends; Cabernet Sauvignon and Malbec, Shiraz Mondeuse and Cabernet, Shiraz and Cabernet Sauvignon.

As is the case with white wine and fish, it is just about impossible to make a serious mistake with red wine and meat (excepting curries of which more later), but it is possible to discover combinations that please your palate.

Poultry and Game.

In this section, we are pleased to debunk one of the old myths of food and wine. To anyone who insists that you drink only white wine with white meat, reply loudly "stuff and nonsense!"

In principle, poultry is best matched to the more full bodied white wines, the vinous or non-aromatic whites; a Semillon or a wood aged Chardonnay. Principles aside, it is perfectly acceptable to drink the lighter reds with poultry, Shiraz and Pinot Noir work very well indeed with roasted chicken or turkey.

Duck is one dish that will even accommodate a sweeter wine, a Crouchen Moselle or a Spätlese Lexia, depending upon the recipe used, or duck á l'orange for example.

When cooking recipes in which meat is only one of the components, you may find a predominant flavour in the dish to match rather than the meat base itself. If, for example, you cook a rabbit in the Greek style, marinated in lemon juice and stewed in red wine and black olives, the mistake would be to treat the rabbit as the delicate dish it is when roasted alone.

Once a rare item on Australian menus and in our kitchens, game such as pheasant, quail and grouse is becoming more available. As this meat is usually cooked after being 'hung' for some time, and is very rich, it is better served in the company of a robust full bodied red, a younger Cabernet Sauvignon or, once again, a peppery Shiraz.

Generally speaking, there is more latitude for experimentation with matching flavours in this category than with any other.

The range of flavours is such that any and every table wine made, may at some stage, be profitably teamed with one or another of the feathered fowl, flying or earthbound.

Semillon

Asian Food.

Gewürztraminer

Perhaps the greatest indication of the changing tastes of a nation is the enormous upsurge of interest in Asian food. This also represents the most difficult area when it comes to finding wines to accompany it; ranging as it does from the fiery curries of India and Sri Lanka to the delicate dishes of Canton and the raw fish of Japan. There is room for bold experimentation and disastrous mistakes.

One of the biggest of these mistakes, to our way of thinking, is to drink red wine with hot curry. Here you will be confronted with the curious spectacle of a winemaker suggesting that you drink beer.

There may be a case for serving a spicy wine, say a Gewürztraminer with a mild and spicy curry, but the heat of a vindaloo will totally obliterate the taste of even the most full bodied red wine.

Here we must report a dissenting voice from the family. One member, who shall go unnamed, advocates accompanying one of the more aromatic Northern Indian curries with a soft and generous Shiraz. This is a recommendation that we pass on to the more adventurous.

In many instances it is a good idea to drink what the locals drink. Sake, for example, is drunk in Japan with the meal. We have heard that a very dry Sherry will take its place where Sake is unavailable, but have not tried it ourselves.

Chinese food is often eaten with aromatic tea. If you would rather drink wine, try Spätlese Lexia, a Gewürztraminer or Dry White Frontignac. Any white wine with enough flavour to match the strong flavours of the food.

Malaysian and Indonesian dishes can be either hot or spicy. Depending upon the chilli factor, the same whites that you enjoy with Chinese food will work with these dishes.

There is also the theory that quantities of chilled white wine will help to quench the fires from these hot dishes. Once again, you be the judge.

Dessert.

That class of wine now known collectively as 'the stickies' here comes into its own.

These are white wines made from grapes left on the vine for as long as the winemaker's nerve holds out, thus developing a very high sugar content, and in some cases, being infected with the fungus known as 'The Noble Rot' or Botrytis cinerea, which has the effect of producing a wine combining a luscious honey flavour on the palate with a crisp finish.

A well made late picked wine should have a delicious sweetness without cloying. The finest examples outside Australia are The French Barsac and Sauternes, such as the famous and pricey Chateau d'Yquem and those German wines cumbersomely named Beerenauslese and Trockenbeerenauslese.

Recent years have seen Australian winemakers developing a high degree of proficiency in producing these excellent wines, and as Australian wine drinkers lose their prejudice against all sweet wines, they are discovering that 'the stickies' are an excellent addition to the table.

We have already recommended these wines for use as aperitifs with hors-d'oeuvres, and with an entrée of pâté or terrine. But they are also wonderful when drunk with desserts made of fresh fruit like pears, peaches, apricots and mangoes. Try a late harvest Orange Muscat and Flora with these dishes.

Any of the late harvest wines combine well with fresh fruit and nuts; the fresh sweetness of a late harvest Rhine Riesling or Spätlese Lexia with peaches, apricots, nectarines, pecans, walnuts and almonds. Or try the Italian combination, pears and pecorino with a late harvest or Noble Riesling

The richer desserts need the assertiveness of the botrytised wines; crème caramel, sicilian cassata cake, any of the sticky tortes or gateaux need a sticky wine. But with chocolate based desserts, only a Liqueur Muscat. This is not a rule, merely a word to the wise.

There are a few taboos at this end of the meal. Be wary of serving wine with flavoured ice cream. Citrus fruits and pineapple will sour the taste of wine, although a mango or rockmelon sorbet with a Noble Muscadelle, for example, will work superbly if you wish to serve an iced dessert.

Finally, and most importantly, let the structure of the preceding meal determine what wine you serve with dessert.

Late Harvest Orange Muscat

Late Harvest Flora

Cheese and Coffee.

Muscat
à petits grains
(Brown Muscat)

Under this general heading, we shall outline some variations on this end of the meal, variations which serve to underline our original assertion that the hidebound traditions of yesteryear if not dead, are, at the very least, not in very good shape.

Traditionally, after dessert, the fortified wines are broken out with coffee and sometimes cheese. The gentlemen retire to the library with cigars and port; the ladies sit by the fire with their embroidery. Dinosaurs have a better chance of survival.

As well as dispensing with such post-prandial segregation, we have also learnt to enjoy other fortified wines with our coffee; the delicious varietal flavours of Muscat and Tokay are a welcome change from the traditional port.

A variation on this theme is to serve cheese and red wine before dessert. Cheese, as you know, is traditionally served with red wine at wine tastings, and for a very good reason. The tannin in red wine has a natural affinity for the protein in cheese; the cheese softens the edge of the tannin and rounds out the taste of the wine.

Yet another variation is to dispense with dessert altogether, and serve red wine and/or dessert wine with a selection of fruits and cheeses; brie and grapes, cheddar and apple, pecorino and pear, ricotta and figs.

After this, if fortified wines are required, serve them with coffee and chocolates away from the dining room table.

At this end of the meal, hopefully you and your guests have been satisfied without being overfed, and have experienced a combination of flavours and tastes that you will remember for a long time to come.

Recipes.

A family that has spent a century making wine has, of course, spent some time cooking food to complement those wines.

And here we have a collection of recipes from the women of the Brown family; Pat Brown, John Brown Senior's wife, June, wife to John junior, Peter's wife Jan, Ross's wife Judy, and Elu, Roger's wife.

Of course they all work in the family business. But more importantly, and perhaps even more than their husbands, they understand and appreciate the finer points of the relationship of wine to food, and how best to achieve the right balances, the right partnerships.

Some of these recipes are old family favourites. Others, like Elu herself, are more recent arrivals from more exotic regions. All have been chosen to complement the wines selected to accompany them.

Pat Brown.

Winter Luncheon.

The diet of our pioneer forebears was based on the very basic foods, meat, flour, sugar, salt, with fruit and vegetables often being rare luxuries, but housewives endeavoured to make the best of that available.

Nowadays in this lucky country, many natural foods are available for most of the year, so planning and preparation of a meal becomes an exciting experience.

An enjoyable meal must appeal to the senses, so that the blending of flavours of the various components is most important, and is enhanced by the addition of complementary flavours of herbs and spices.

The presentation of the meal is equally important and involves the use of the colour of vegetables or fruit in an artistic way.

The table setting of attractive linen, cutlery and glassware, provides the environment to feature artistry of the chef, and finally the choice of appropriate wines to complement the food flavours, will ensure a happy event for the guests.

Menu.	Wine Selection / Choice.
Upon guest arrival	Gleuwein.
Hors-d'oeuvres. Avocado and Smoked Salmon Rolls.	Dry White Frontignac or Chardonnay.
Soup Butternut soup, topped with cream and sprinkled with pumpkin seeds.	Sylvaner or Gewürztraminer.
Main Course Chicken Parmesan with Basil, Crunchy sweet & sour rice. Snow peas & carrots.	Chenin Blanc or Rhine Riesling.
Cheese Platter	Meadow Creek Cabernet Sauvignon & Shiraz.
Coffee With Ginger Slice.	Very Old Tokay or Very Old Port.

Gleuwein
Hot mulled wine
(12 serves)

1½ cups boiling water
½ cup sugar
½ lemon, sliced
3 sticks cinnamon
3 whole cloves
1 bottle red wine
(light or medium bodied)

Combine boiling water, sugar, lemon, cinnamon and cloves. Stir until sugar dissolves. Add wine and simmer for 20 minutes. (DO NOT BOIL). Strain and serve hot with a sprinkling of nutmeg.

Avocado and Smoked Salmon Rolls
Prepare, cover, refrigerate up to 3 hours before serving.

1 small avocado
125g ricotta cheese
¼ cup sour cream
1 teaspoon lemon juice
salt and pepper
200g sliced smoked salmon
¼ cup chopped fresh dill, or parsley

Combine avocado pulp, ricotta cheese, sour cream, lemon juice and salt and pepper in processor, process until smooth.

Spread avocado mixture onto slices of smoked salmon, roll up like swiss roll, cut into 5cm lengths. Secure each roll with a toothpick. Spread ends of each roll with avocado mixture, dip into chopped dill or parsley.

Makes about 20.

Butternut Soup

1kg butternut pumpkin, 1 large onion
1 large carrot, 2 sticks celery
2-3 tablespoons oatmeal
2 chicken stock cubes
salt, cayenne to taste

Cook all vegetables in sufficient water to cover, for half an hour. Put through blender. Return to saucepan. Mix in oatmeal which has been blended with a little water. Boil soup with oatmeal for 10 minutes, add salt, cayenne and chicken cubes. Lastly add sufficient milk to bring soup to creamy consistency. Hot milk is better.

Test and taste, add salt with care, do not boil after adding milk.

Serve garnished with a teaspoon whipped cream, sprinkle of chives and a few pumpkin seeds, if possible.

Chicken Parmesan with Basil
(Serves 6)

6 Chicken breasts
1½ cups fresh breadcrumbs
¾ cup parmesan cheese
1½ teaspoons chopped parsley
4 rashes bacon, 120g butter,
2 large cloves garlic
1½ teaspoons worcestershire sauce
¾ teaspoon dry mustard

Combine breadcrumbs, cheese, parsley in a bowl, cut bacon finely, fry until crisp. Drain.

Add bacon to breadcrumb mixture, melt butter, add crushed garlic, worcestershire sauce, and dry mustard. Mix well.

Dip chicken fillets into butter mixture and place in shallow oven proof dish. Press crumb mixture on top of each fillet. Bake uncovered in moderate oven 20-25 minutes. Serve with Basil sauce.

Basil Sauce

Combine in saucepan,
½ cup oil
1 crushed garlic clove
½ cup wine vinegar
1 cup fresh basil leaves
½ cup cream
salt and pepper

Stir until heated through. Add yoke 1 egg, stir until thickened. <u>Do Not Boil.</u>

Ginger Slice
No baking

1 cup dates, stoned and chopped
1 tablespoon mixed peel
90g preserved ginger, drained and
    chopped
150g butter
⅓ cup raw sugar
3 cups cornflakes

Heat all ingredients together, do not boil. Press into a swiss roll tin.

Icing

250g cooking chocolate
80g unsalted butter

Melt butter and chocolate together. Spread over top of slices.

Crunchy Sweet and Sour Rice

4 cups cooked brown rice
1 small red pepper, chopped
2 green shallots, chopped
⅓ cup canned water chestnuts, sliced

Sweet and Sour Sauce

1 tablespoon cornflour
½ cup chicken stock
½ cup canned pineapple juice
1½ teaspoons white vinegar
1 teaspoon sugar
1 tablespoon peanut butter

Combine hot rice with pepper, shallots and water chestnuts. Stir in hot sweet and sour sauce. Blend cornflour with stock. Add pineapple juice, vinegar, sugar and peanut butter. Stir over heat until mixture boils and thickens, reduce heat, simmer one minute.

June Brown.

Summer Luncheon.

I enjoy preparing a dinner or luncheon party for a small number of guests. My general rule is simplicity of preparation and simplicity of presentation. With this thought in mind I try to choose recipes which can be prepared well ahead of the meal time, leaving me more time to enjoy my guests and giving me greater confidence knowing that each course is well planned and practically ready to be served.

It is also important to take into consideration the blending of flavours which are to be served with particular wines. The dominance of one flavour can over power a wine or even a whole meal. Again simplicity comes into my choice of flavours.

The summer luncheon meal which I have planned is neither too rich in flavour nor too large in quantity. I consider a summer luncheon needs to be light because of the warm weather and light because it is served in the middle of the day. With these thoughts in mind I have chosen lighter styled wines to suit the menu.

Menu.	Wine Selection / Choice.
Soup Summer corn and bacon Accompanied by wholemeal cheese loaves.	Chardonnay or Sauvignon Blanc.
Main Course. Spinach pancakes with tomato-onion sauce, served with tossed salad. Accompanied by wholemeal cheese loaves.	Tarrango or Pinot Noir.
Dessert. Fresh fruit fondue with cream sauce.	Koombahla Late Harvest Rhine Riesling or Spätlése Lexia.
Coffee With shortbread. Mineral water on the table throughout meal.	

Wholemeal Cheese Loaves
This recipe makes 3-4 small stick loaves

3 cups wholemeal plain flour
3 cups plain white flour
2 tablespoons gluten flour
2 teaspoons salt
30g butter, melted
1 teaspoon raw sugar
50g fresh yeast, crumbled
2 cups water ⎫
1 cup milk ⎭ *combine and warm*
25mg tablet ascorbic acid, crushed

Add all ingredients in given order to large bowl. Mix quickly with hand or wooden spoon. When dough leaves side of bowl turn onto floured surface, knead until smooth, divide into 3 or 4 equal portions. Roll out each portion, sprinkle 3 tablespoons grated tasty cheese over dough. Roll up as for a swiss roll and turn under. Place in narrow well greased loaf tins, or on scone tray, leave to rise until double in size, approx. 1 hour. Note: an excellent hint is to put tin with dough in it into plastic bag and place in warm sun, this promotes rising.
Cook in oven 170° for 20-30 minutes. To test bread, tap crust which should sound hollow when cooked. Putting a pan of water into oven as bread bakes helps prevent crust becoming too hard. The loaves can be made the previous day and re-heated, they will also freeze very satisfactorily.

Summer Corn and Bacon Soup
450g can creamed corn
2 cups chicken stock
30g butter
4 shallots
3 bacon rashers
¾ cup cream

Combine creamed corn and chicken stock, heat gently. Melt butter in pan, add chopped shallots, finely chopped bacon, cook until bacon is crisp. Purée shallots and bacon in blender, add corn mixture and blend until smooth. Cool, stir in cream, refrigerate until well chilled. Garnish with finely chopped shallots or chives. Makes 6 small serves.

Spinach Pancakes with Tomato-Onion Sauce
⅔ cup plain flour
2 eggs
2 teaspoons oil
2 ⅔ cups milk
250g packet frozen chopped spinach

Sift flour, add eggs and oil, gradually stir in milk. Thaw and drain spinach, stir into batter. Pour ¼ cup batter in greased, heated pan, cook slowly until golden brown underneath, turn and brown other side. Put tablespoon of filling in centre of each pancake, roll up. Place pancakes into greased, shallow oven-proof dish, cover and bake in moderate oven 15 minutes. Makes 12 pancakes.

Ricotta Cheese Filling
2 tablespoons pinenuts
300g ricotta cheese
3 tablespoons grated parmesan cheese
salt and pepper

Stir pinenuts over low heat until golden, cool. Beat ricotta cheese with parmesan, pinenuts, salt and pepper.

Tomato-Onion Sauce
425g can whole tomatoes
30g butter or margarine
1 tablespoon garlic chives
1 onion
salt and pepper

Sauté chives and finely chopped onion in butter, add mashed (or blended) undrained tomatoes, bring to boil, reduce heat and simmer 10-15 minutes.
To serve: Pour tomato sauce over 2 pancakes on each plate. Serves 6. Accompany meal with tossed salad.
Pancakes and filling can be prepared some hours before meal or even stored overnight.

Fresh Fruit Fondue
Selection of fresh fruits:
raspberries, blackberries, cherries, strawberries, rockmelon, pear, fig, apricot, grapes, banana, plum, kiwifruit.
Any combination of these is suitable using 4 or 5.
My favourites are apricots, strawberries, bananas, rockmelon and kiwifruit.

Cream Sauce
1 cup natural yoghurt
½ cup cream
⅓ cup coconut
3 tablespoons chopped walnut
3 tablespoons smooth apricot jam
3 teaspoons finely chopped preserved ginger

Whip cream, combine all ingredients. Slice fruit, arrange on individual plates or central plate. Serve cream sauce in bowl for guests to serve themselves or in small individul bowls. Dip fruit portions into cream sauce.
Serves 6

Shortbread
250g butter
1 teaspoon vanilla
⅓ cup castor sugar
2¼ cups plain flour
¼ cup ground rice or rice flour

Cream butter and vanilla until light and fluffy, gradually beat in sugar until creamy.
Work in sifted dry ingredients, knead well on lightly floured surface until smooth. Form into biscuits and mark with fork, or press dough into shortbread moulds and turn out. If using moulds dust with a mixture of flour and castor sugar.
Put onto greased oven tray and cook in slow oven for approximately 45 minutes, or until just turning golden brown.

Barbera

Jan Brown.

Summer Barbecue.

I really enjoy entertaining in our home. My husband Peter and I plan the menu together so that the wines and food complement one another.

I enjoy setting the dining table to suit the occasion trying always to keep it simple, but elegant! We don't have large dinner parties, only six or eight friends at a time as we feel this gives us more time to spend with our guests. A dinner party with friends is important so only the best will do – beautiful wine and good food.

I firmly believe that when preparing a meal you must balance the courses so that your guests go home satisfied, not over indulged! When planning the meal I always take into account the colour combination of the food, as visual effect is most important and helps with the enjoyment of the meal.

This, of course is not the only thing to consider – find a good butcher too! I am fortunate living where I do as my butcher – Bob – always supplies me with tender and succulent meat.

Our two daughters, Eliza and Angela enjoy cooking too so perhaps one day they will be competent enough to cook for our dinner parties.

Menu.	Wine Selection / Choice.
Entrée Platter of fresh seafood, prawns, lobster pieces, oysters, calamari and blanched scallops served with a dill dressing.	Dry White Frontignac.
Main Course Rump Steak Shaslicks served with spinach, pinenut & mushroom salad and bacon-topped potatoes. (A wine sauce served in a jug).	Koombahla Pinot Noir.
Cheese Platter With walnut bread and fresh fruit.	Sauvignon Blanc.
Dessert Strawberry Meringue Crown.	Spätlese Lexia.
Coffee Home-made Chocolates.	

Platter of Fresh Seafood

To use as hors-d'oeuvres and entrée. My family loves seafood. This is very easy to prepare and a great favourite with friends and family alike.

Prawns, lobster pieces, oysters, calamari and scallops (blanched for a few minutes). Serve these with a bowl of dill dressing.

Dill Dressing

(serves 8)

300ml sour cream
1 cup mayonnaise
1 cup french dressing
2 tablespoons chopped chives
2 tablespoons chopped fresh dill
Whisk all ingredients together.

Beef Shaslicks

A very tasty dish and a change from the normal barbeque style. Cut as much rump steak into pieces as required. Thread meat and small onions, pieces of green capsicum, cherry tomatoes and mushrooms onto skewers and place on barbeque. Prepare wine sauce and use to baste and serve with shaslicks.

Wine Sauce

1 onion finely chopped
2 crushed cloves garlic
2 tablespoons salad oil
1 cup red wine
¼ cup dry sherry
¼ cup soy sauce
2 tablespoons tomato puree
1 tablespoon peanut butter

Sauté onion and garlic in oil until golden. Add wine, sherry, soy sauce and tomato purée. Bring to boil and simmer until reduced by a third. Add peanut butter, mix thoroughly.

Green Spinach or Silverbeet, Pinenut & Mushroom Salad

This is beautiful, quite tangy and crunchy. Very refreshing with the shaslicks.

250g mushrooms
½ cup vinaigrette
1 bunch endive
1 head lettuce
spinach or silverbeet, washed, stems removed and large leaves shredded
2 tablespoons toasted pinenuts
½ cup chopped spring onions
1 avocado sliced

Marinate mushrooms in vinaigrette for 2 hours. Just before serving, tear endive and lettuce into pieces and place in a bowl with mushrooms and spinach or silverbeet. Add pinenuts, spring onions and avocado. Toss together and add more vinaigrette if necessary.

Bacon-Topped Potatoes

(Serves 6)

This recipe is very tasty and the topping can be prepared ahead of time. Very popular with family and friends.

As many medium potatoes as required
oil, salt
3 bacon rashers, finely chopped
1 onion chopped
diced capsicum
3 green shallots, chopped
1½ cups grated tasty cheese
2 tablespoons grated parmesan cheese
2 tablespoons chopped parsley

Pierce potatotes all over with fork, rub with oil and salt. Bake in moderate oven for 1 hour. Sauté bacon and onion until bacon is crisp. Add capsicum, shallots, cheeses and parsley, stir 1 minute. Cut potatoes in half and top with bacon mixture.

Cheese Platter

Cambazoli
Brie
Tasty
water biscuits
walnuts bread slices

Serve these on a large glass platter surrounded with figs, dates, grapes and slices of apple.

Walnut Bread

My family loves cheese. This bread adds an interesting texture combined with the cheese and fruit. Delicious!

220g ricotta cheese
140g brown sugar
3 eggs
110g walnuts
220g self raising flour
1 teaspoon baking powder
½ teaspoon salt

Grease and flour a loaf tin. Cream ricotta cheese and sugar and beat in the eggs. Stir in walnuts. Sieve in the flour, baking powder and salt and fold into mixture. Turn into tin, bake in moderate oven almost one hour. Leave to cool in tin and then turn out.

Strawberry Meringue Crown

This is a highlight to a barbecue, easy to prepare and always enjoyed. It can be prepared a couple of hours before serving.

Meringue
4 egg whites
pinch salt
8 tablespoons (not heaped) castor sugar

Beat egg whites with the salt until stiff. Gradually add castor sugar and beat until mixture is glossy and holds stiff peaks. Place small dessertspoonfuls on a well-buttered tray. Place in a slow oven 140°C until firm and dry. When cooked remove & loosen from tray. Leave to cool and store in an air-tight tin. Makes approximately 36 meringues.

Select a platter about 30cm in diameter. Spread a thin layer of cream over the base. Arrange a circle of meringues around edge of platter, fill the centre with 1 punnet strawberries, hulled. Keep aside 4 meringues to be used for the top. Pair the other meringues together with generous spoonfuls of cream. Place these over the berries and around the edges using more cream to hold them so they look like a pyramid completely covering the strawberries. Place in refrigerator whilst preparing melted chocolate to decorate finished dessert.

60g dark chocolate
15g unsalted butter

Melt chocolate, add butter, this makes chocolate easier to use. Place chocolate mixture into piping bag with a plain tube. Quickly pipe all around so chocolate forms lines and pieces over outside. Chill until chocolate is set.

Finish the meal with percolated coffee and my daughter Eliza's homemade chocolates.

Judy Brown.

Winter Dinner.

I like nothing better than a dinner party with friends. My mother, who was a most gracious hostess, a wonderful cook, and who loved to entertain, stressed upon me the importance of doing this with style, but also with individuality. Everyone has their own way of doing things, consequently, a dinner party should be a reflection of the personality of the host and hostess; from the table setting and the flowers, to the choice of menu through to the wines.

I love to experiment — new recipes, new ideas and new styles of cuisine. When planning a dinner party, I usually decide on the main course first, and then choose the entrée to complement this.

Dessert is always a problem. Ross and I are not dessert eaters, so I tend to choose something that I know the guests will enjoy, something that will go with the wine to be served, and something I can make beforehand.

I enjoy the preparation of food so I tend to choose recipes that can be prepared beforehand so I can spend the maximum time with my guests at the table. In the menu I have chosen, all courses can be prepared before the guests arrive. With Hors-d'oeuvres, the Caviar Profiteroles can be assembled as can the Marinated Scallops, which then only need be put under the griller.

The entrée need only be cooked in the oven ½hr before serving, and the Basil Sauce could be prepared that morning. The veal could be prepared the night before, with only the vegetables needing immediate attention.

Dessert and the Chocolate Macaroon slice, once again could have been prepared well in advance.

Because we like wine, I like to present a varied menu so as the different grape varieties and wine styles are seen at their best when matched with food.

Menu.

Hors-d'oeuvres.
Caviar Profiteroles
Marinated Scallops in bacon.

Entrée
Prawn Mousse
with fresh basil sauce.

Main Course
Veal rolls with two stuffings:
1. Spinach / Pinenut.
2. Apricot / Walnut.

Stir fried vegetables- Snow Peas,
Zucchini, Carrots, Red Pepper Mushrooms,
Chats & Mint.

Cheese / Fruit.

Dessert.
Individual fruit flans.

Coffee
Chocolate Macaroon slice.

Wine Selection / Choice.

Flor Fino Sherry or
an old Rhine Riesling.

Sauvignon Blanc or Chardonnay.

Merlot or Merlot blend or Shiraz.

Koombahla Cabernet Sauvignon
or Shiraz, Mondeuse & Cabernet.

Noble Riesling or Late Harvest
Orange Muscat & Flora.

Liqueur Muscat or Very Old Tokay.

Caviar Profiteroles
Makes 30 savouries

Choux Pastry
I usually make this in the food
processor as a time saver.
½ cup cold water
60g butter, cut into small pieces
½ cup flour
¼ teaspoon salt
2 large eggs

Filling
6 hard boiled eggs
salt and pepper
1 tablespoon finely grated white onion
2 tablespoons well flavoured
mayonnaise
3 teaspoons finely chopped parsley
sour cream for topping
1x45g jar each red and black caviar
 smoked salmon can be used to replace
or alternatve with caviar.

This savoury is based on tiny choux pastry puffs filled with egg and topped
with caviar. Recipe makes 30 profiteroles but half the filling can be made,
the remaining puffs frozen for another time. Before using thaw puffs for
about 4 to 5 minutes in moderate oven 200°C (400°F).
Place cold water in saucepan, add butter, bring to boil making certain butter
is melted when water boils. Sift flour and salt onto piece of paper. Remove
pan from heat, add all flour. Stir well, return to heat. Cook until it leaves
sides of pan and begins to film base of pan, which usually takes a minute.
Cool for two minutes.
Beat eggs with fork, gradually add to pastry, beating well. This can be done
by hand, or using a mixer or processor. Beaten well with a wooden spoon
ingredients should mix well in a few minutes. All egg may not be needed,
mixture should hold a shape when lifted with spoon.
Grease baking tray with butter. Put mixture into pastry bag with large plain
tube, pipe small portions out, about size of 20¢ piece, or place teaspoons of

mixture onto tray. Use egg mixed with teaspoon of milk to glaze tops of puffs. Bake puffs in moderate oven 200°C (400°F) for about 20 minutes, reduce heat to 180°C (350°F) and leave for further 5 to 10 minutes. When cooked and crisp remove from tray, pierce side of each one to release steam, otherwise they will soften. Turn oven off, leave door open, allow puffs to dry and cool for 10 minutes. They can be kept in airtight tin for up to a week. If they do soften, place in oven for a few minutes, they will become crisp again. Mash hard boiled eggs with salt, pepper, onion, mayonnaise and parsley. Mixture should be moist and well seasoned. Cut top from each choux puff, using a teaspoon or coffee spoon fill each with egg mixture, mounding slightly. Place dob of sour cream on top, then some caviar of each colour. Puffs can be filled about 30 minutes before serving, but no sooner or they will soften.

Note: Ideally the caviar is added almost at last moment, especially if using black caviar, as colouring make the sour cream a grey colour.

Marinated Scallops in Bacon

½kg scallops
15 slices bacon
Marinade: ¼ cup oil
      1 tablespoon soy sauce
      2 cloves garlic, crushed
      juice 1 lemon
      ground pepper
      dill

Place scallops in bowl with marinade, allow to stand approximately 2 hours. Stir occasionally. Drain scallops, wrap in ½ slice bacon and secure with a toothpick. Place under griller, turn once until bacon is crisp.

Quantity of hors-d'oeuvres depends on scallop size.

Prawn Mousse with Fresh Basil Sauce

750g fish fillets eg. John Dory, Gem Fish, Whiting
500g green prawns, shelled
2 egg whites
1 cup cream
2 teaspoons tomato paste
cooked prawns for decoration (approx. 2 each)

Fresh Basil Sauce

30g butter
¼ cup water
½ cup dry white wine
½ cup cream
2 tablespoons lemon juice
1 cup fresh basil leaves

(Fresh Basil Sauce cont.)

2 teaspoons cornflour, add to sauce if not thick enough

Cut skin from fillets. Lightly grease a 3 cup, 20cm wide, 5cm deep savarin tin (or 20cm ring tin). Line tin with fillets, dark side up, thick end to centre, overhanging outside and inside rims of tin. Reserve remaining fillets to enclose and cover mousse mixture before baking.

Devein green prawns, place in processor until smooth. With motor running add egg whites, cream and tomato paste, process until smooth, spoon mixture into tin.

Place remaining fillets over mousse, fold ends over top to enclose mousse mixture. Place tin in baking dish filled with enough hot water to cover halfway up side. Bake in moderate oven 25 minutes, or until firm to touch. Pour off excess liquid, invert onto serving plate, remove tin. Serve with fresh basil sauce and cooked prawns.

Fresh basil sauce: combine water, butter, wine, cream and lemon juice in pan, bring to boil, reduce heat, simmer uncovered 2 minutes. Pour sauce into blender, add basil leaves, blend until smooth. Return sauce to pan, stir in blended cornflour if necessary.

Stir constantly over medium heat until sauce boils and thickens. Note: Mould can be prepared 2 hours before cooking. Serve once cooked as dish is not suitable for reheating. Basil sauce can be made many hours ahead and reheated before serving.

Veal Rolls with Two Stuffings
16 slices prime veal
16 slices good ham
1 tablespoon oil
20g butter
1 cup dry white wine
Lay veal between greaseproof paper and beat gently to flatten. Cover each piece with slice of ham. Prepare stuffings, divide between veal slices, 8 spinach, 8 apricot. Secure each with cocktail stick.
Heat oil and butter in large frying pan, add rolls until lightly browned. Transfer to oven dish, pour in wine, cover and cook gently in oven, turning once, for 20-25 minutes or until tender. Transfer rolls to oven proof dish to keep warm. Bring pan juices to boil and reduce.
Cut each veal roll into slices, arrange on plates alternating stuffings for visual effect. Spoon over sauce and serve with vegetables.

Spinach and Pinenut Stuffing
½ bunch spinach, chopped finely and cooked
½ cup pinenuts
4 tablespoons grated parmesan cheese
1 clove garlic, crushed
¼ cup fresh breadcrumbs
1 egg
Mix all ingredients together.

Apricot and Walnut Stuffing
½ packet dried apricots, chopped
½ cup walnuts or almonds, chopped
2 tablespoons chopped parsley
black pepper
¼ cup fresh bread crumbs
1 egg
Mix all ingredients together.
Note: Stuffed veal rolls can be made day before until the cooling and kept in fridge, wine will marinate the meat.

Stir Fried Vegetables
Using: *snow peas*
 mushrooms
 baby carrots
 red pepper
 zucchinis
 any vegetable in season
Peel and pre-cook carrots, ensure they remain firm. In wok or large frying pan heat 3 tablespoons good oil. In order add zucchini, baby carrots, mushrooms, red pepper, snow peas. Heat through only and serve immediately.

Chats and Mint
Choose 2 chats or gourmet potatoes per person. Boil in water with 4 sprigs of mint, do not remove skins. When cooked remove mint, toss lightly in butter if desired. Serve.

Individual Fruit Flans
This elegant French dessert has a shell of tender biscuit pastry filled with creamy custard and topped with colourful fruits covered with a glistening brandied-apricot glaze. Fruits in season can be used in place of cherries, apricots, strawberries suggested here eg. kiwi fruit, raspberries, cantelope etc.

Pastry

1 cup plain flour
1 teaspoon icing sugar
¼ teaspoon baking powder
pinch salt
90g butter
1 egg yolk
1 teaspoon lemon juice
1 teaspoon water approx.

Fruit Topping

500g black cherries, pitted
500g ripe apricots
1 punnet strawberries

Glaze

2 tablespoons apricot jam
1 teaspoon brandy

Glaze: Put jam and brandy in saucepan, heat gently until boiling, push through sieve for a smooth glaze.

Sift dry ingredients into bowl, rub in butter until mixture resembles coarse breadcrumbs. Mix to firm dough with lightly beaten egg yolk, lemon juice and water. If necessary add little more water. Knead lightly on floured board, wrap in plastic, refrigerate 30 minutes.
Roll pastry on lightly floured surface, cut 8 circles, lift gently over rolling pin into flan tins. Ease pastry into sides of tins with fingers, press lightly into grooves. Run rolling pin over top of tin firmly to cut off excess pastry and neaten edges. Prick base with fork. Bake in moderate oven 10 to 15 minutes or until pale brown, allow pastry to cool in tin.
When completely cold, fill bases of pastry with cold custard, arrange fruit decoratively over custard, brush fruit well with warm apricot glaze.

Confectioners Custard

3 eggs
90g castor (superfine) sugar
3 tablespoons flour
430ml (scant 2 cups) milk
few drops vanilla essence

Blend eggs, sugar and flour. Boil milk and pour onto egg mixture. Stir well. Return to pan, bring to boil and simmer 2 to 3 minutes until thick. Remove from heat, stir frequently so skin does not form, add vanilla essence.

Chocolate Macaroon Slice

A saddle tin is a fluted semi-circular cake tin available from cookware shops. However, a bar tin, base measures 7cm x 25cm, would be a good substitute.

185g dark cooking chocolate
125g red glace cherries
30g angelica or green glace cherries
30g sultanas
30g mixed peel
185g (2 cups) coconut
½ cup castor sugar
2 eggs

Line saddle tin with aluminium foil so that it protrudes 5cm over each end of tin. Chop chocolate roughly, sprinkle over base of tin. Place in moderate oven until just melted, spread chocolate evenly over base of pan. Chop angelica or cherries, mix with sultanas and peel, sprinkle mixture evenly down centre of chocolate.
Mix coconut, sugar and eggs, distribute evenly over fruit mixture, level top. Bake in moderate oven 30 minutes or until lightly browned. Cool, refrigerate over night, turn out, wrap in aluminium foil and store in refrigerator. Serve in thin slices.

Elu Brown.

Summer Dinner.

This is one of my dinner menu plans that I recently used when entertaining some friends midweek.

This dinner menu is very convenient for entertaining during busy work periods when I don't have much time for a meal which requires a lot of last minute preparation.

Being a relatively inexperienced cook and one who enjoys being with my guests, doesn't allow me time to prepare a more complicated meal.

However, with this dinner menu, most of the preparation can be done well in advance with the exception of some small tasks which will only take a short time.

A couple of important points for this menu to be successful are that the meat must be of top quality and must be tied correctly.

The Prosciutto may have to be ordered from your shop ahead of time. Pay close attention in selecting a crisp ripe melon as an over ripe one will be a disappointment.

Menu.	Wine Selection/Choice.
Appetiser Stuffed Mushrooms.	Sylvaner or Chenin Blanc.
Entrée. Prosciutto and Melon	Dry White Frontignac or Rhine Riesling.
Main Course. Beef Peron (Scotch Fillet with pink peppercorns).	Cabernet Sauvignon or Shiraz.
Dessert Zabaglioni.	Late Harvest Orange Muscat & Flora or Spätlese Lexia.
Coffee. With Chocolate Mints.	Liqueur Muscat or Very Old Port.

Stuffed Mushrooms
(serves 8)

18 mushrooms (1½ inch)
½ cup chopped scallops
3 lettuce leaves
1 lemon

Wash dry and peel the mushrooms if necessary. Chop scallops — stuff the mushroom caps with this mixture; refrigerate.
When ready to serve place under hot griller for 5 to 8 minutes.
Serve on bed of lettuce with slices of lemon on side.
I sometimes serve slices of strawberries around this dish for colour, and decoration.

Proscuitto And Melon
(serves 8)

1 cantelope
8 small lettuce leaves
8 slices proscuitto (Italian ham)
2 Lemons

Place lemons on dish, slice cantelope into 8 pieces, place on top of lettuce and place slices of proscuitto on melon. Slice lemons into 8 slices and serve on side dish.
With my Latin influence I find the addition of a small colourful flower to the side of the dish adds contrast.

Beef Peron
Scotch fillet with pink peppercorns.

2 Scotch fillets
1 jar pickled pink peppercorns
½ cup cream
Port

Trim and tie two splendid scotch fillets, pan brown very well, sprinkle peppercorns over meat, splash sizzling meats with port and allow to flame. Settle the meat overnight in the refrigerator, sprinkled with all the pan juices plus more port. Remove fillets to oven dish and reheat in a high oven for 30 minutes. On stove top reduce pan juices and darken with cream, serve as sauce.
I recommend that you ask your butcher to tie the fillets as they do a better job, and this saves time. Serve with vegetables of your choice. I usually serve potatoes in their jackets with baby carrots and string beans.

Zabaglione
(serves 4)

5 egg yolks
¼ cup castor sugar
½ cup Marsala
¼ cup dry white wine

Combine egg yolks and sugar in top of a double saucepan. Beat for a few minutes, off heat, with rotary hand or electric mixer until well combined. Put mixture over simmering water. Beating well, gradually mix in half Marsala, half white wine. Slowly beat in the remaining Marsala and wine. Beat constantly for about 10 minutes, until thick and creamy. If mixture adheres to side of pan, quickly remove from heat and beat vigorously with wooden spoon — especially around base. Pour into individual dishes. Note: — In place of Marsala, any favourite liqueur can be used. Zabaglione makes an excellent topping for fresh fruit, or pour it warm over icecream.

Coffee
With chocolate mints or milk chocolate.

Cabernet Franc

Ruby Cabernet

Local dinner for 6.

This meal is a combined Brown family effort, utilising the marvellous fresh produce of the Milawa district and the surrounding countryside.

Using only available, fresh and seasonal produce is perhaps the single most important principle behind the finest French and Italian cooking. The French call this cooking 'à la marché', or from the market.

Indeed many domestic and professional European cooks refuse to plan a meal until they have inspected the markets, and selected that which is at its peak, only those foods which are freshest.

Although these local delicacies are from Milawa and its surrounds, the same principle applies to cooking 'à la marché' wherever you live.

Menu.	Wine Selection / Choice.
Hors-d'oeuvres	
Mustard and egg crudités.	Sauvignon Blanc.
Entrée	
Trout with lemon parsley butter.	Rhine Riesling or Semillon.
Main Course	
Glazed rack of lamb à la Milawa.	Shiraz.
Scalloped potatoes.	
Green beans & mushrooms.	
Baked herb tomatoes.	
Australian Cheese Board.	
Tasty cheddar, Brie, Gouda.	Cabernet Sauvignon & Shiraz.
Dessert.	
White chocolate mousse with fresh fruit sauce. Choice of blackberries, strawberries, kiwifruit, brambleberries, raspberries.	Noble Riesling. Late Harvest Orange Muscat & Flora.
Coffee	
Served with toffee dipped grapes.	Very old Tokay.

Many of the ingredients used in the local dinner are readily available in the district surrounding Milawa, and in Autumn, which is our vintage season.

Mustard and Egg Crudités

125g cream cheese
½ cup mayonnaise
½ cup natural yoghurt
125g grated cheddar cheese
2 teaspoons 'French-style' prepared mustard
3 hard boiled eggs
1 tablespoon chives
1 tablespoon parsley
salt and freshly ground pepper

Put all ingredients into blender and process until mixture is a smooth consistency. If mixture is too thick add cream to adjust consistency. Serve in a bowl on a platter surrounded by sliced raw vegetables of your choice.

Trout with Lemon Parsley Butter

When cooked this way there is no need to scale fish as skin will peel away easily after cooking.

6 small trout
120g butter
2 teaspoons grated lemon rind
1 small garlic or 1tblsp garlic chives
salt and pepper
2 tablespoons chopped parsley
2 tablespoons lemon juice

Wash and dry trout, place in aluminium foil and wrap tightly. Foil must be large enough to enclose fish completely. Bake on tray in moderate oven for 20 minutes. Fish can be barbecued this way if wrapped in double thickness foil.
Blend softened butter, lemon rind, garlic/chives, parsley and lemon juice. Season with salt and pepper, mix well. Serve fish topped with butter, or serve butter in a bowl on table.

Glazed Rack of Lamb à La Milawa

6 racks of lamb
3 tablespoons oil
5 tablespoons lemon juice
1 tablespoon soy sauce
4 tablespoons honey
2 teaspoons rosemary
¾ cup water
2 tablespoons chopped mint
2 tablespoons brown vinegar
1½ tablespoons sugar
2 tablespoons water (extra)

Trim chops, remove excess fat. In bowl combine oil, lemon juice, soy sauce and honey. Prick chops all over with metal skewer, add to marinade, leave 2 hours, turning occasionally. Drain, reserve marinade for basting.
Place chops in baking dish, press a little rosemary on each, brush with a little marinade. Bake in moderate to hot oven 30-45 minutes depending on how pink, brush frequently with pan juices. After 30 minutes pour in water to prevent juices burning.
When cooked, remove chops, place pan on top of stove and reduce liquids to ½ cup, strain into small saucepan. Combine mint, sugar, extra water, vinegar, add to pan, bring to boil, reduce heat for 2 minutes, pour sauce over chops.

Scalloped Potatoes

Using 1 medium potato per person. Grease large deep dish, slice potatoes, line dish with layer, sprinkle gourmet black pepper, lots of garlic salt, grate tasty cheese over this, pour cream on top. Repeat layers, sprinkle tasty cheese and parmesan cheese on top. Cook in moderate oven approx. 1 hour. Add a little milk if more liquid required.

Green Beans and Mushrooms

Cook amount of beans required until just done. Slice quantity of mushrooms, cook slowly in butter until they change colour, keep warm. Combine beans and mushrooms and serve.

Baked Herb Tomatoes

6 Tomatoes
1 tablespoon lemon juice
salt and pepper
15g (½oz) butter
2 teaspoons chopped parsley
1 teaspoon chopped chives
2 teaspoons basil

Slice off stem end of tomato, place in greased oven proof dish, sprinkle lemon juice over top, then salt and pepper. Bake in moderate oven 10 minutes. Remove from oven, dot each tomato with butter, sprinkle combined parsley, chives and basil on top, bake for further 5 minutes.

White Chocolate Mousse with Fresh Fruit Sauce

140g white chocolate
60ml cold milk
1 level teaspoon gelatine
1½ tablespoons brandy
1½ tablespoons cold water
¾ cup (190ml) thickened cream
2 egg whites
6 timbales of 100ml capacity

Fresh Fruit Sauce

1½-2 tablespoons castor sugar
2-3 tablespoons water (if necessary)
1 tablespoon cream
Suggested fruit: blackberries, strawberries, kiwifruit, brambleberries, raspberries.

Lightly grease timbales with peanut or safflower oil. Melt chocolate in bain-marie, add cold milk little by little, beating constantly. Mix brandy and water, stir in gelatine and dissolve over heat in another bain-marie. Cool both mixtures, add gelatine to chocolate, stir in unbeaten cream. Beat egg whites to soft peaks, whisk into chocolate mixture, strain into timbales, refrigerate over night.
Vitamize fruit, sweeten with sugar according to taste. Add water and cream, vitamize until you have thick purée, strain mixture and refrigerate. Dip timbales quickly in warm water, unmould onto serving plates, surround with sauce.

Toffee Dipped Grapes

250g grapes
2 cups sugar
1½ cups water

Wash and dry grapes, cut into small bunches, make sure grapes are perfect and firmly attached to stems.
Combine sugar and water in pan, stir over heat until sugar dissolves, bring to boil, do not stir and boil rapidly for about 10 minutes or until toffee is light golden brown. Allow bubbles to subside, quickly dip grapes into toffee using tongs, place on aluminium foil-covered tray to set.

Grape Varieties.

Cabernet Sauvignon

This classic grape is responsible for many of the distinguished reds produced by the world renowned Chateaux of the Bordeaux districts – Médoc, Graves, St Emilion and Pomerol among them. Not only has it adapted to Australian conditions, but in the hands of our own world renowned winemakers, it has taken on a character all its own.

As befits a classic, it has a long and well recorded pedigree. Pliny the Elder (A.D. 23-79) described a vine almost certainly the Cabernet during that period when Bordeaux was a part of Roman Gaul.

The vine is strong growing, with semi upright shoots, and the mature foliage is dark green. Medium to small long conical clusters of small tough skinned and heavily pigmented berries mature late, and upon maturity, have a characteristic pungent aromatic flavour.

Even so, a native Bordelais, tasting the huge wines traditionally produced from his favourite grape in this country, would suffer from culture shock of the palate. There are a variety of reasons for this.

Firstly, Cabernet Sauvignon, of all the red wine grapes, is perhaps most affected by variations in growing conditions; altitude, climate and soil all affect the flavour of the grape, and the resultant wine. Too hot, and the wine will be unbalanced, too cold, thin and astringent. Even under ideal conditions, variations in soil, for example, will introduce nuances of flavour and aroma.

Then there are winemaking styles. A winemaker with a grape is like an artist with a blank canvas; each one will 'create' a wine in his own style, based upon individual preferences and local conditions. For many years, the Australian style of Cabernet Sauvignon showed more body than fruit. Today, that style is changing to allow the fruit (varietal) flavour to predominate. However, many of our older Cabernets, drinking today, were made in that older style.

And most French Cabernet Sauvignon is blended, which has a softening effect. Australian winemakers also blend, most notably with Shiraz.

But the daddy of them all is the big Aussie Cabernet Sauvignon, oak and bottle aged for at least five years, at its best displaying an astonishing depth of varietal flavour, richness, complexity and a bright red colour. A huge mouthful of a wine.

Such a wine deserves nothing less than to be the centrepiece of a memorable meal, and should be accompanied by rich and powerful friends.

A roast of beef or pork, a turkey with chestnut stuffing, a hearty daube, casserole or cassoulet; any of the game birds, pheasant, grouse or wild duck.

More simply, a slab of Stilton and a ripe old cheddar on a board with some water biscuits, a bottle opened an hour beforehand, and fine company may be all that is needed.

A truly great wine needs neither elaborate accompaniment, nor indeed, very much in the way of conversation. Let it speak for itself.

Chardonnay

Here is a grape that represents the most astonishing success story in recent Australian winemaking history. In just under ten years, Australian plantings of Chardonnay have increased eightfold.

In France, Chardonnay is used in Champagne, counterpointing the depth of the Pinot Noir with its delicacy. The wines of Chablis are pure Chardonnay, as are many of the Burgundian whites, Meursault and Montrachet included.

The vine is vigorous, with large dark green roughened leaves. The berry cluster is small, cylindrical and compact, the berries small, round, thin skinned, and, although possessed of a distinctly fruity flavour, are without aroma.

Very broadly, white wine grapes can be divided into three categories based on aroma.

The floral aromatics include the Rieslings, Gewürztraminers and Muscats. From harvest, these grapes exhibit a rich aroma, redolent of the heady scent of flowers.

The non floral aromatics, Sauvignon Blanc and Colombard among them, give a herbaceous aroma, sometimes referred to as a capsicum or, more prosaically, a cabbage aroma.

The vinous, or non aromatic varieties, Chardonnay, Marsanne and Semillon for example, have little varietal aroma and are described by the winemaker as neutral.

Quite obviously, different techniques of winemaking are needed for each of these types. The floral grapes are treated in order to capture as much of their heady aroma as possible in the wine. With these varieties, fruit is generally uppermost on the palate.

The non floral aromatics, tending towards a dryness or flintiness on the palate, are again treated to capture as much as possible of their aroma.

The vinous grapes need entirely different treatment. As a young wine, Chardonnay is generally dull and plain. When aged in oak, the wine matures, and develops astonishing depth of colour, complexity and aroma.

Strangely enough, this does not just mean the aroma of the wood. What the wood seems to do is to react in some alchemical way to highlight the fruit character of the grape.

A winemaker can get carried away with the taste of wood. The wise winemaker uses wood like the good chef uses salt; the flavour should not be obvious, but should add complexity and depth of aroma and taste.

The very best Chardonnays display all these characteristics in well balanced proportions; flintiness, mellowness, and the distinctive varietal character from a gentle association with wood.

The acidity of a Chardonnay, its pleasing dryness, make it, like the Sauvignon Blanc, an ideal seafood wine. Its austerity combined with the ocean tang of fresh untouched oysters is one of the finest food and wine associations possible. Indeed, Chardonnay is as good for drinking with any crustacean as seawater is for growing them. Lobster, crab, yabbies, Balmain or Moreton Bay Bugs, all go well with this full bodied white.

Rhine Riesling

This noble grape is thought by some ampelographers (scientists of the origination and classification of the vine) to have originated on the banks of the Rhine, by others to be that grape called Argitis by the Romans, cultivated by them from the third century on the banks of the Rhône.

Its tightly packed golden russet speckled berries grow on a moderately vigorous vine with rough dark green leaves. It is not an easy vine to cultivate, and yields its floral aromatic varietal flavour more readily in cooler climes.

Under these conditions, the wine will be pale green gold when young, exhibiting a definite varietal flavour and aroma, and what has been described as an acid backbone. With age, the acid will soften, the colour deepen to a rich gold and the varietal flavour intensify and fill out.

In its other incarnation, as the Noble Riesling, it is a luscious honeyed wine of intense flavour and aroma, with a surprising acid finish. For this wine, legend tells us, we must thank the Bishop of the little German town of Fulda in 1775.

It appears that the good Bishop was also a vineyard owner, and, in that role, had forgotten to pass on to his vineyard manager the order to pick the grapes (another version of the story has the messenger waylaid by bandits). The manager waited, and waited, and, finally, fearing the impending arrival of a thirsty Bishop to an empty cellar, picked the few remaining grapes, which by this time were covered with fluffy grey fungus and pink spots. To his joy and relief, the resultant wine was possessed of an intensity of flavour and depth of sweetness never before tasted. The hapless winemaker had accidentally discovered the beneficial effect of Botrytis cinerea (in English the Noble Rot, in French pourriture noble, in German Edelfaule) on the Rhine Riesling grapes.

Filaments from this fortuitous fungus penetrate the soft skinned berries, thus evaporating away the water and concentrating the sugar level of the grape, imparting to the resultant wine a taste described by winemakers as 'botrytised', and by winedrinkers as 'bloody marvellous'.

In Australia the first recorded occurrence of Botrytis cinerea, naturally an accidental event, and dependent upon weather and the presence of the spore, was recorded by winemaker John Charles Brown in the family vineyard in 1934. In 1962, the Brown Brothers produced Australia's first Noble Riesling.

What all this means of course is that with these three styles of Rhine Riesling, you may begin, continue and end a meal with wine from a single grape. Noble Riesling, although most often drunk as a dessert wine, is used by the French to accompany pâté or terrine as an entrée.

On the other hand, a fresh and lively young Rhine Riesling complements with a seafood or vegetable entrée.

A more mature version of the wine is the perfect partner for a main course, a roast chicken or duck.

Finally, with a dessert of fresh mangoes, or peaches and ricotta cheese, the Noble Riesling is nothing short of sublime.

Pinot Noir

If grapes wore clothes, this silky specimen would look right at home in top hat and tails. In any of its roles, as a varietal red, or as the major constituent of Champagne, this is one swellegant, elegant grape.

Even the invading Romans, inclined towards ripping out the local vines and planting their own, formalised the supremacy of the Pinot Noir upon colonising Burgundy by banishing its rival, the Gamay, from the district.

Not a vigorous grower, and even when fully developed, not a highly productive vine, it has a sparse appearance, with bright green roughened three to five lobed leaves. Its small cylindrical berry clusters are well filled to compact with medium sized oval deeply pigmented grapes which ripen early, and tend toward sunburn.

All the great Burgundies, and they are the masterpieces of the French wine world, wines like Gevrey-Chambertin, Vosne-Romanée, Aloxe-Corton and Pommard are produced solely from this grape. Two thirds of the grapes used to make Champagne are Pinot Noir a 'black' skinned grape with a white pulp.

Until recently it has not been an extremely popular variety in Australia, more interested as we were in the 'big' reds; as late as 1984, only 50 hectares were planted, compared with 4000 in California.

This was also probably due to the genetic weakness of the variety which can cause complications; an early ripener, it can overripen fast; not being a vigorous grower, it doesn't produce a large leaf canopy to protect the berry from the sun.

Solving such problems in viniculture and winemaking has been the adventure and the challenge in Australian winemaking since the 1960s. The uniformly high standard and unparalleled variety of wines available here are evidence of our success.

One example of this is the superb Pinot Noir being produced. The increased plantings of this grape point to its continued growth in popularity.

This is not surprising; not only have our winemakers succeeded particularly well with this grape, but as our tastes develop, to include all the styles of red wine available, from the full bodied through medium to light, a medium bodied style like the Pinot Noir will find more and more favour.

The best Australian Pinot Noir, grown only in cool climate vineyards, is a soft and subtle wine, with an attractive plum-like aroma and a similar cherry plum flavour, with a hint of sweetness.

It is this appealing fruitiness which makes it the perfect partner for pasta dishes with meat sauces, with cold meats, cold veal dishes and cold roast beef. It is also said to be the only red wine to be drunk with the flying game birds; duck, squab, pigeon and pheasant.

The medium body and full fruit flavour also works well with those dishes from the 'nouvelle cuisine' which combine meat and fruit; such dishes as lamb with apricots, veal with cherry sauce, even old favourites like pork and apple sauce.

Chenin Blanc

Here is an example of a Sleeping Beauty, a grape which has waited patiently for the kiss of modern technology to bring it to full fruited, full bodied life in the late twentieth century.

The Chenin Blanc grow in large compact conical clusters on a vigorous semi upright vine. The berry is tough skinned, oval, and at harvest, has a rich fruity floral aromatic flavour with good acidity.

From its legendary beginnings as a planting on the banks of the River Loire by St Martin (the 4th century patron saint of innkeepers and drunkards) the Chenin Blanc, or Pineau de la Loire in France, has produced light graceful wines.

Wines that have often been compared to the very pretty country that nurtured the grape, the garden of France, and, for centuries, the summer residence of French Royalty.

These wines include the still and sparkling Vouvrays and the sweet, fruity (often botrytised) wines of Anjou and Touraine. They are fresh scented and exhibit an orchard of tastes, variously described as peachlike, apricotlike and hazelnutty. They are often disparagingly dismissed as 'picnic wines'.

However, with the advent of the cold fermentation process, this grape has been given a new life, and new found depth of varietal character.

Very simply, by cooling the must (grape juice before fermentation) fermentation is slowed down, and the winemaker can preserve and balance the fruity components of the taste, components which would otherwise be broken down and dissipated by a warmer and faster fermentation.

The Chenin Blanc made in Australia by this process is a far cry from the French wines from the same grape. It is in every way a more robust and flavoursome wine, with an almost perfect sugar/acid balance. Which does somewhat increase its versatility as a table wine.

Because of this outstanding balance, it works extremely well as an aperitif, chilled and served with canapes and hors-d'oeuvres, serving to stimulate rather than satiate the appetite.

As an entrée wine, it drinks exceptionally well with the nutty oily taste of avocado, and with any combination of seafood and avocado, or indeed with any seafood and tangy sauce entrée.

Try it also with quiche or vegetable tarts, light chicken dishes, salads from the nouvelle cuisine or stir fried Chinese chicken dishes.

Here is yet another example of the Australian winemaker taking a completely new look at a grape, and coming up with a totally new category of wine.

Sauvignon Blanc

A curious grape, difficult to handle, with rather fussy tastes in soil, this aromatic nonetheless yields rewarding wines for the patient winemaker.

In its region of origin, Bordeaux, centuries of experience have resulted in two quite distinct styles of wine being produced from the grape.

The most distinctive style of Sauvignon Blanc is grown in the very cool region of the Loire Valley in the North of France. Here the wines are fresh and herbaceous, aged without wood and drunk young to highlight the outstanding freshness of the variety.

The other name for this grape, used in California, and to a lesser extent in Australia, Fumé Blanc, or white smoke, refers not to the taste but to the grey smoky bloom that covers the ripening berries.

The vine is vigorous and early ripening, its leaves bright grassy green and three to five lobed. The berries grow in compact cylindrical bunches, are greenish yellow with a light bloom, soft texture and display a rich and characteristic flavour at maturity.

That's the problem with Sauvignon Blanc. That powerful flavour can be, quite literally, a knockout. It has been said of this grape that it is a bare knuckle boxer rather than a master of karate.

Here in Australia, it definitely needs to be handled with kid gloves and grown in a cool climate. Then, it will produce a crisp dry wine with good varietal flavour and quite intense herbaceous aroma, sometimes compared to the smell of capsicum.

If ever there was a wine to be served with seafood, here it is. The aroma, crisp clean taste, acid finish and pale green gold colour all combine to make it look and taste exactly right with our abundant seafood.

A cool crisp Sauvignon Blanc with a plain grilled lobster, a plate of blue swimmers or a butter brushed and grilled schnapper may be, for many, the perfect Australian summer luncheon.

It will take some bottle ageing, and indeed this should intensify its positive characteristics and round off a little of the acid edge.

Young or old, here is an honest and straight forward wine, most comfortable in the company of food prepared and served in a similar manner.

Gewürztraminer

A full flavoured floral aromatic variety far easier on the Australian palate than the tongue; pronounced 'Ge-verts-tram-eener'.

This particular grape is an aromatic clone of the Traminer grape ('Gewürz' meaning 'seasoned' or 'spicy' in German), one of the oldest of the European grapes, whose origin is lost in time, although intelligent speculation would place them somewhere near the Italian Tyrolean town once called Tramin. Today, the finest wines from this grape in Europe are made in Alsace on the French German border.

It grows on a vigorous vine with large dark green rough surfaced leaves. The clusters are small and compact. The berry is small, oval with a tough thick skin and is unique in that its mature colour is russet pink with brown undertones. At maturity, the fruit has a pronounced spicy flavour and aroma.

This varietal flavour is intensified when the vine is grown under cool climate conditions. It follows then, that the wine made from this grape is not a subtle one: it has variously been described as one of the world's most distinctive tastes, exotic, fascinating and exciting.

Yet it is exactly this full frontal flavour and aroma that makes the Gewürztraminer an ideal accompaniment for rich food.

Say Gewürztraminer to an Alsacien, and he will reply 'sauerkraut'. In Alsace, and in France generally, this rich cabbage concoction served with spicy sausages is the traditional partner to the wine.

In Australia, it makes an ideal companion for Asian food, for the subtler curries, Chinese dishes, and those Indonesian and Malay dishes in which chilli has not been used as a weapon.

It makes a most agreeable summer aperitif, especially before luncheon, served with olives, cheese and spicy salamis.

It's well to remember that a good Gewürztraminer will darken in colour, and further intensify in flavour and aroma after a few years in the bottle. If you can stand such power, and resist the temptation to drink immediately, the rewards are worth the wait.

Whether you drink it today or tomorrow, with sauerkraut or with sate, you will drink it with a good measure of pleasure.

Mondeuse

Mondeuse is the mystery grape; rarely encountered alone in a bottle, grown only in a relatively small area of North Eastern Victoria and a tiny corner of France near the Italian/Swiss border where it is known as an après ski wine. It is most definitely not the name on every winelover's lips.

Large loose bunches of these intensely black grapes hang from a vigorous vine with sparse three-lobed rough light green leaves. The berry is round to oval, small, ripens late and is high in tannin.

In Savoie, where it is also known as the Parsagne, it is used to produce a small number of relatively undistinguished wines (the Savoyards may disagree), Arbin, Montmélian and St-Jean-de-la-Porte among them. Savoie, hardly one of the major wine producing areas of France, was only given Appellation Contrôlée status in 1970.

So what is the secret of the dark stranger? Like the life of the party, who may not be much fun when encountered alone, the Mondeuse is a superb mixer.

Earlier in this section, we introduced the analogy of the winemaker and the artist in discussing wine styles. The same analogy is useful in discussing blending.

The artist, beginning with a clean palette, blends colours to achieve the right balance in a painting, taking into account such factors as personality, harmony and the emotion to be conveyed.

The winemaker, beginning with a clean palate, blends grapes in order to achieve the right balance in a wine, taking into account fruit, tannin, acidity, body, aroma and longevity.

In the case of a blend of Shiraz, Mondeuse and Cabernet, each grape supplies a different quality.

The Cabernet Sauvignon, its complexity and marvellous varietal flavour; the Shiraz adds generous soft fruit quality; and the Mondeuse abundant tannin, acidity and long life. For its ability to add age to a wine, it has been called the 'Golden Wedding Grape'.

A blend is made by picking the grapes separately, making a wine from each, then blending them in exactly the right proportions. Here, the palate of the winemaker is used to achieve the perfect balance of the best qualities of each variety.

This particular blend, Shiraz, Mondeuse and Cabernet, is a full bodied full flavoured red wine which will require food of a similar stamp.

Like a straight Cabernet Sauvignon, this blend will suit rich casseroles, or a hearty red wine beef stew, always remembering to add generous dollops of the same wine to the dish.

And, like all fine old red wines, it will further demonstrate the truth of the old saying 'what a friend we have in cheeses'. A red wine of good tannin like this is particularly pleasing with mature cheese.

Tarrango

F. LONGHURST

And now for something completely different. A grape variety bred in Australia specifically for Australian conditions which, surprisingly, produces a wine remarkably similar to a famous French light red.

The Tarrango grows in well filled bunches on a vigorous cane with a light green, three to five-lobed medium smooth leaf. The berries, larger than normal, are black with a characteristically deep red seed.

It is a cultivar: that is, a plant produced under cultivation. A deliberate cross between the Portuguese Touriga – a port wine variety – and the high yielding Sultana.

The idea of developing cultivars is almost as old as winemaking itself. In the traditional winemaking countries, they are bred to adapt vines to local conditions. In Germany, more than half the wine produced is from cultivars. There, they are developed for increased yield, flavour and early ripening ability to suit the colder Northern European conditions.

In Australia, breeding has aimed at developing grapes suited to the hot inland irrigation areas. The qualities looked for were late maturity, high acidity, good sugar acid balance and resistance to rain damage.

In 1975, Allan Antcliff of the CSIRO Division of Horticultural Research at Merbein in Victoria released the Tarrango grape, named after a nearby locality.

It was an instant success. In 1978, a wine made from this grape won a silver medal in the small vineyard class in light dry reds in the Canberra Wine Show. In a blind taste testing conducted by a wine magazine, a Tarrango outpointed two wines from the French Beaujolais region.

For that is the style of Tarrango. A light, dry red wine with an extremely attractive reddish purple colour, a fresh fruity aroma and a flavour of ripe red currants. It is at its best drunk fresh, young and chilled, like a classic Beaujolais.

This is a radical departure from the usual style of Australian red wines. A red wine at its best in the year of production? Heresy! A chilled red wine? Blasphemy! Yet, such a wine has a remarkably broad appeal, not only to red wine drinkers, but to those of us who would normally never drink red.

It is the perfect summer luncheon wine. It may be drunk with fish, with cold meats, for example with a cold veal and tuna fish mayonnaise, with cold pasta salads, with fresh cheese and fruit, or ham. In Paris there is a bar that serves only the finest ham and goat's cheese on crusty bread with Beaujolais. Try Tarrango with ricotta and figs, or fetta and grapes.

It may be drunk with a westering sun on a hot summer's evening on the deck of a boat or the shady verandah of a country house. It is cooling, and thirst quenching, the perfect reward at the end of a long hot day at the beach.

Above all, Tarrango is a welcome additon to the remarkable range of flavours available to the Australian wine drinker, whose choice is already the envy of the world.

Shiraz

Without knowing it, lovers of Australian red wines owe a debt of gratitude to the labours of a war-weary Crusader.

In 1224, Gaspard de Sterimberg, repulsed by the atrocities of the Albigensian wars, retired to a hillside in the Rhône Valley, built a small hermitage, and devoted his life to the worship of God and the cultivation of the Shiraz grape.

Under the ministration of de Sterimberg and his descendants, wine made from these vines, known collectively as Hermitage, reached a peak in the 19th century, when they were considered the peers of the first growth Bordeaux and the finest Burgundies.

And thus the Shiraz grape (often called Hermitage to this day) was considered worthy of transport to Australia.

Indeed, Shiraz has been called the founding grape of the Australian Red Wine industry, so well suited is it to Australian conditions (10,000 hectares planted here as opposed to just over 3000 in France). The typical Australian red wine style of the fifties (red brown verging on black in colour, distinctive roasted aroma and jammy fruit flavours) was the taste of a late-picked Shiraz.

And so, as our tastes developed and refined, and the taste of European migrants impinged upon our own, so too did the style of the Australian Shiraz.

Today's finest Shiraz is a deep red purple in colour, displaying clean, rich fruit both on the palate and the nose, the distinctive peppery varietal flavour and the sweet spice of new oak. An infinitely more complex wine than the chewy toffee reds of yesterday.

Australia is still one of the few wine growing countries outside of Europe to have extensive plantings of Shiraz. The American grape called Petite Syrah (Syrah being the European name for the Shiraz grape) is in reality either a clone of the European Syrah or a selection of another Rhône Valley variety, Durif.

A vigorous grower, with small to medium-sized oval berries growing in long and cylindrical bunches with dark russet green leaves, its versatility allows it to be used alone, blended, or even in the production of fortified wines.

Because the intensity of the resultant wine's colour, tannin and acid increases or decreases as the climate it is grown in varies, the winemaker has the opportunity to experiment with different styles using the same grape. This is particularly relevant in the north east of Victoria because of the diversity of meso-climates.

Such an elegant wine is the perfect companion to roast lamb, pork or duck; but save your older bottles for the rich game birds, pheasant, squab or grouse.

If the Crusades achieved nothing more than the introduction of the Shiraz grape to Australia, it will be argued by some wine lovers that they were well worth it.

Semillon

Enter Semillon, the chameleon, the mystery grape. In France, the major constituent of one of the lushest and most exotic dessert wines on earth; in Australia, producing extraordinary dry table wines reminiscent of the finest white Burgundies.

Indeed the best of the Australian Semillons – full flavoured, round on the middle palate, soft finishing – are said to capture the elusive varietal characteristics of this non-aromatic grape (the same category as Chardonnay) in a way unequalled elsewhere in the world.

Like Chardonnay, the Australian Semillon needs some bottle aging. As a young wine, although pleasant enough drinking, it shows little of the distinction that is to come. Time is needed to develop the rich golden colour, the full varietal complexity, to work the magic mingling of grape and oak.

This ability to grow in the bottle is shared with its French relatives from Bordeaux, where it is the major white variety, and plays a starring role in the legendary Sauternes, Chateau d'Yquem.

It is not the only variety used in the botrytised dessert wines of Sauternes (being blended with Sauvignon Blanc and Muscadelle); indeed, nowhere in France is Semillon made as a sole varietal.

It is too early to tell whether any of our Semillons will reach the age of 180 as did a 1784 Chateau d'Yquem, opened and tasted at Christie's in London in 1964, to be pronounced "...perfect in every sense; colour, bouquet and taste." We must wait.

While we do, we might like to ponder some of the other mysterious aspects of the Semillon: the uncertainty surrounding the origin of its name, and the continuing cases of mistaken identity and misnaming in Australia.

Does the name Semillon come from the obscure Saint Emilion? Or the Bordeaux district St. Emilion? If the latter, why are there no plantings there when we know it has been grown in Sauternes since the first century?

Since arriving in Australia, it has been variously misrepresented as Chenin Blanc in Western Australia, Crouchen and Riesling in South Australia

To add to the confusion, in the Hunter Valley, home to most of the 2600 hectares planted in Australia, it is sometimes known as Hunter River Riesling.

It is a vigorous variety, with conical, well-filled bunches of small round to oval berries and medium five-lobed rough and undulating leaves. One final mystery: while only the white fruited form is known in France, in Australia, red-fruited forms have been found.

And what to eat with this master of disguises? Well, in its Australian incarnation, it shares Chardonnay's affinity for seafood in all its forms. But save your grand old Semillons for something special. A rich bouillabaisse, for example, or a seafood ragout.

What is most easily understood about this wine is the reason for its increased utilisation by Australian winemakers (especially in North East Victoria) and its growing acceptance among Australian wine drinkers. It is, quite simply, a wonderful wine with food.

Index.

Graciano

Recipes

Bastardo